NATURE HEALS

HIKING IN NATURE

BY ABBY COLICH

BLUE OWL BOOKS

TIPS FOR CAREGIVERS

Social and emotional learning (SEL) helps children manage emotions, learn how to feel empathy, create and achieve goals, and make good decisions. One goal of teaching SEL skills is to help children care for themselves, others, and the world around them. The more time children spend in nature and the more they learn about it, the more likely they will be to appreciate it and receive its emotional benefits.

BEFORE READING

Talk to the reader about hiking. Explain that it is different from walking outside but that both activities can be beneficial.

Discuss: Do you like to go for walks outside? What do you like about them? Have you ever been hiking? Where did you go?

AFTER READING

Talk to the reader about how walking outside, hiking, or just spending time in nature makes him or her feel. Discuss the benefits of feeling connected to nature.

Discuss: How do you feel after hiking or walking outside? Do you feel better after spending time outside?

SEL GOAL

Children may struggle with processing their emotions, and they may lack accessible tools to help them do so. Explain to children that spending time in nature can help people feel good. Hiking or walking are easy ways to spend time in nature. They are also great forms of exercise, which can improve one's mood. Encourage readers to hike or walk outside to help them relax or calm down when they are upset.

TABLE OF CONTENTS

CHAPTER 1

LET'S GO ON A HIKE!

Have you ever been hiking? Maybe you've hiked on a trail in the woods or on a path in a city park. No matter where you go, hiking is great exercise.

Hiking is good for your body. It also lets you spend time outside. Spending time in nature is good for your mind. When you hike or exercise, your brain releases **endorphins**. These chemicals help improve your mood.

Hiking can help you feel more connected to nature. It can help you be more **mindful**. When you are mindful, you are **focused** on what is happening in the moment. This can help you feel calmer.

CARE FOR THE TRAIL

When you go hiking, be mindful of your surroundings. Stay on the trail so you don't hurt the living things around you. Take any trash with you. Don't feed the animals or take any plants.

CHAPTER 2

PLAN YOUR HIKE

Hiking requires just a little planning and a few supplies. First, have an adult help you plan where to go. If you are new to hiking, find a path or trail that is not too difficult. Look for one that doesn't have too much **elevation**. A paved path will be easiest to walk on.

Pack a water bottle. If you are going on a long hike, you may want to pack snacks. Bring a flashlight, first-aid kit, and extra layers. A backpack can hold your supplies.

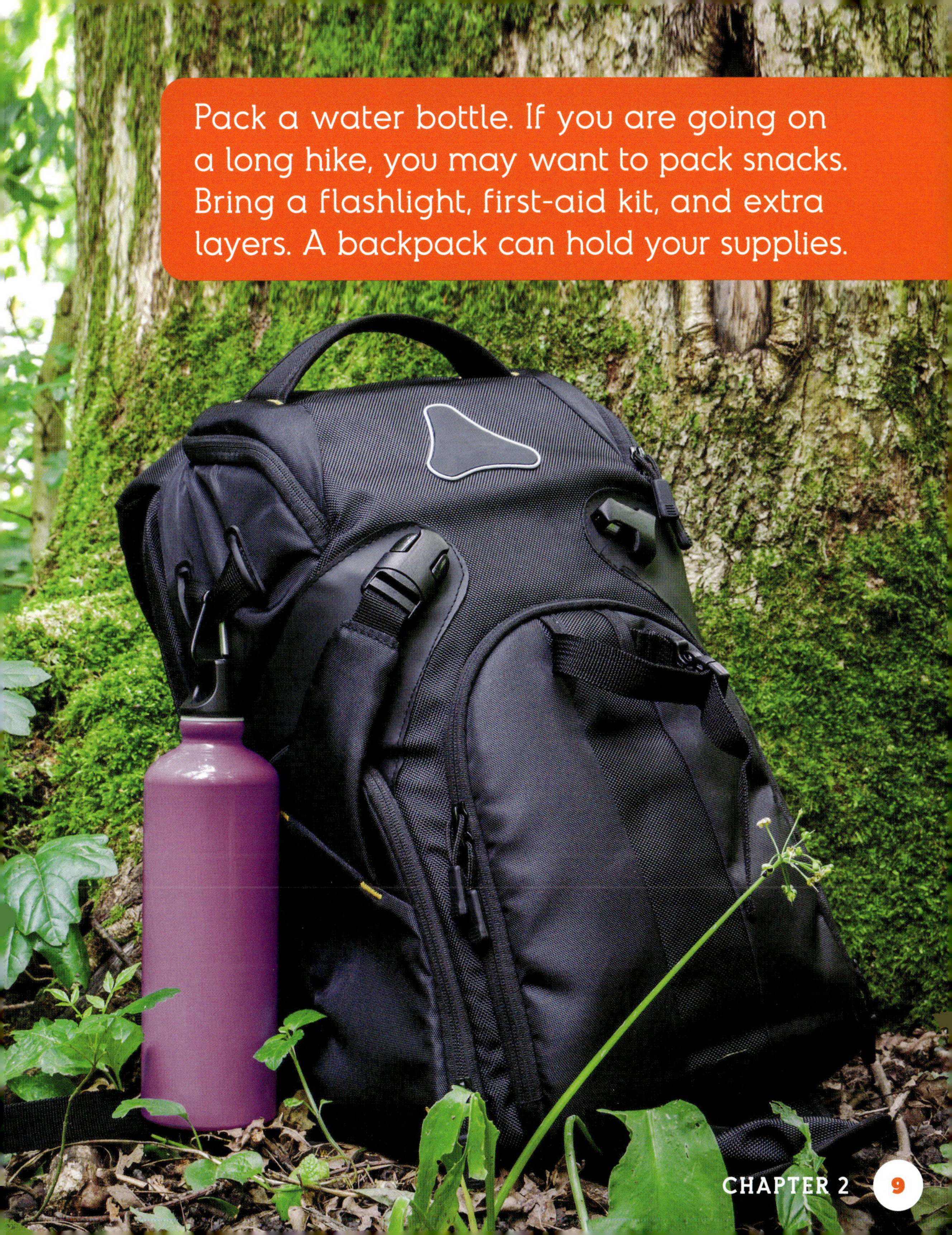

Check the weather. Make sure you are dressed right for the temperature. Do you have the right boots or shoes for the **terrain**? Wear sunscreen. You may also need bug spray.

LET OTHERS KNOW

Never hike alone. Before you go hiking with your group, let someone else know where you will be. Let them know when you expect to be back, too.

CHAPTER 3

MINDFUL HIKING

Before you start your hike, set an **intention**. Do you want to feel more relaxed? Do you want to challenge yourself to try something new? Maybe you want to forget something that is bothering you. If your mind starts to wander on the hike, come back to your intention.

Stay positive. **Encourage** the people you are hiking with. Some people may be slower, but be **patient**. Remember that you all have the same **goal** to finish your hike together.

Think about how your body feels. If you feel stiff, try doing some stretches. While hiking, make sure you don't slouch. Keep your back straight and shoulders down. Good **posture** can help you stay **alert**.

MANTRAS

A **mantra** can help you stay focused. Try repeating a phrase to yourself as you hike. "I am strong" and "I can do this" are two options.

Don't worry about speed. Just walk at a steady pace. Can you hear a **rhythm** as your feet hit the ground? Does the rhythm change depending on the terrain? Focus on the beat. It can be calming.

Try to find a rhythm with your breath, too. Pay attention to how the air moves in and out of your body.

MINDFUL WALKS

If you can't go hiking, try a walking **meditation**. Focus on each step. Do you feel the muscles in your legs working? Do you feel your breath moving in and out of your nostrils?

If your mind starts to wander, stop for a break. Notice the **scenery** around you. How does the sun or wind feel on your skin? How does the fresh air smell? Do you hear animals or other noises?

When you are finished with your hike, focus on how you feel. Do you feel calm? Was the hike difficult? Hiking can be hard work, but it is very rewarding. Take time to feel proud of what you accomplished. Then set a goal or intention for your next hike!

GOALS AND TOOLS

GROW WITH GOALS

Hiking is a great way to exercise and feel more connected to nature. If you can't go hiking, try going for a walk outdoors.

Goal: Try to get outside every day. If you can't go for a hike or walk, kicking a soccer ball around or just breathing fresh air can be good for you, too.

Goal: Before you begin a hike or walk, decide you are going to count the number of butterflies or birds you see. Or look for a certain kind of plant or a different animal. A goal like this will help you stay focused.

Goal: Keep a hiking journal. Write down where you go and how far you hike. Also include your intentions and how you felt before and after your hike.

MINDFULNESS EXERCISE

If you are stressed or anxious, go for a hike or walk. Focus on each step you take. Try repeating "up, down, up, down" to yourself as you take each step. Find a rhythm as you walk. Is the rhythm soothing? Then spend a few moments focusing on your breath as you move. How do you feel when you are finished?

GLOSSARY

alert
Able to think clearly and notice things.

elevation
The height of a place.

encourage
To give someone confidence, usually by using praise and support.

endorphins
Substances created by the brain that reduce pain and cause pleasant feelings.

focused
Concentrated on something.

goal
Something you aim to do.

intention
Something you mean to do.

mantra
A sound, word, or phrase that is repeated while meditating or practicing mindfulness.

meditation
The act of thinking deeply and quietly as a way of relaxing your mind and body.

mindful
A mentality achieved by focusing on the present moment and calmly recognizing and accepting your feelings, thoughts, and sensations.

patient
Able to put up with problems or delays without getting angry or upset.

posture
The way in which the body is positioned when sitting or standing.

rhythm
A repeated pattern of sounds or movements.

scenery
Outdoor scenes or views that are pleasing to look at.

terrain
The features of the surface of a piece of land.

TO LEARN MORE

FACT SURFER

Finding more information is as easy as 1, 2, 3.

1. Go to www.factsurfer.com
2. Enter "**hikinginnature**" into the search box.
3. Choose your book to see a list of websites.

INDEX

Blue Owl Books are published by Jump!, 5357 Penn Avenue South, Minneapolis, MN 55419, www.jumplibrary.com

Library of Congress Cataloging-in-Publication Data

Names: Colich, Abby, author.
Title: Hiking in nature / by Abby Colich.
Description: Minneapolis: Jump!, Inc., 2021.
Series: Nature heals | Includes index. | Audience: Ages 7–10
Identifiers: LCCN 2020041885 (print)
LCCN 2020041886 (ebook)
ISBN 9781645278405 (hardcover)
ISBN 9781645278412 (paperback)
ISBN 9781645278429 (ebook)
Subjects: LCSH: Hiking–Psychological aspects–Juvenile literature. | Nature–Psychological aspects–Juvenile literature.
Social learning–Juvenile literature. | Mindfulness (Psychology)–Juvenile literature.
Classification: LCC GV199.52 .C69 2021 (print) | LCC GV199.52 (ebook) | DDC 796.51–dc23
LC record available at https://lccn.loc.gov/2020041885
LC ebook record available at https://lccn.loc.gov/2020041886

Editor: Eliza Leahy
Designer: Michelle Sonnek

Photo Credits: Brocreative/Shutterstock, cover; amriphoto/iStock, 1; RG-vc/Shutterstock, 3; Dmytro Zinkevych/Shutterstock, 4; michelangeloop/Shutterstock, 5; Pixel-Shot/Shutterstock, 6–7; narikan/Shutterstock, 8; Cristi Croitoru/Shutterstock, 9; JGA/Shutterstock, 10–11; Creativa Images/Shutterstock, 12; AnnaStills/Shutterstock, 13; Ksana Durand/Shutterstock, 14–15; Vadym Lesyk/Shutterstock, 16–17; Romiana Lee/Shutterstock, 18–19; bonandbon/Shutterstock, 20–21.

Printed in the United States of America at Corporate Graphics in North Mankato, Minnesota.